Classifying Living Things

Nonflowering Plants

Francine D. Galko

Chicago, Illinois

www.heinemannraintree.com
Visit our website to find out
more information about
Heinemann-Raintree books.

To order:

☎ Phone 888-454-2279

💻 Visit www.heinemannraintree.com
to browse our catalog and order online.

Edited by Catherine Clarke and Claire Throp
Designed by Victoria Bevan and AMR Design Ltd
Original illustrations © Capstone Global Library LLC
Illustrations by Carrie Gowran
Picture research by Hannah Taylor
Originated by Steve Walker
Printed and bound in China by Leo Paper Group

13 12 11 10 09
10 9 8 7 6 5 4 3 2 1

Library of Congress Cataloging-in-Publication Data

Galko, Francine.
  Nonflowering plants / Francine Galko.
    v. cm. -- (Classifying living things)
Includes bibliographical references and index.
Contents: The variety of life -- Nonflowering plant divisions
-- The plant kingdom -- Liverworts and hornworts -- Mosses
-- Whisk ferns -- Club mosses, spike mosses, and quillworts
-- Horsetails -- Ferns -- Seed plants -- Conifers -- Other
gymnosperms -- Organizing nonflowering plant.
  ISBN 978 1 432923 60 0 (Hardcover) --
  ISBN 978 1 432923 70 9 (Paperback)
1. Cryptogams--Juvenile literature. [1. Plants. 2. Cryptogams.]
I. Title. II. Series.
  QK505.5.G35 2003
  586--dc21
                    2003004978

Acknowledgments

We would like to thank the following for permission
to reproduce photographs:

ardea.com pp. 7t (Francois Gohier), 16 (Bob Gibbons); Corbis
pp. 4 (Bill Ross), 5 (Mark Karrass), 7b (Micro Discovery), 13
(David Muench), 19 (Hal Horwitz), 20 (Robert Glusic), 21,
27 (Wolfgang Kaehler), 22 (Phil Schermeister), 23 (Gunter
Marx Photography), 24 (Darrell Gulin), 25 (Ecoscene/Andrew
Brown); FLPA pp. 26 (David Hosking), 28 (Konrad Wothe);
Getty Images p. 12 (Taxi/David Maitland); naturepl p. 14 (Doug
Wechsler); Photolibrary pp. 9 (Juan Carlos Munoz), 11 (Harold
Taylor), 17 (Carolina Biological), 18 (Photolink/S. Solum);
Science Photo Library p. 15 (Andrew Syred).

Cover photograph of Kamahi tree ferns in Westland National
Park, New Zealand, reproduced with permission of ardea.
com/Jean Paul Ferrero.

We would like to thank Ann Fullick, Jack Shouba, botany
instructor at the Morton Arboretum, and Kenneth R.
Robertson, Illinois Natural History Survey, for their
invaluable assistance in the preparation of this book.

Contents

Some words are shown in bold, **like this**. You can find out what they mean by looking in the glossary.

The natural world is full of an incredible variety of **organisms**. They range from tiny **bacteria**, too small to see, to giant redwood trees over 100 meters (328 feet) tall. With such a bewildering variety of life, it's hard to make sense of the living world. For this reason, scientists **classify** living things by sorting them into groups.

Classifying the living world

Sorting organisms into groups makes them easier to understand. Scientists try to classify living things in a way that tells you how closely one group is related to another. They look at everything about an organism, from its color and shape to the **genes** inside its **cells**. They even look at **fossils** to give them clues about how living things have changed over time. Then the scientists use all this information to sort the millions of different things into groups.

Scientists don't always agree about the group an organism belongs to, so they collect as much evidence as possible to find its closest relatives.

The redwood trees in this forest are nonflowering plants.

From kingdoms to species

Classification allows us to measure the **biodiversity** of the world. To begin the classification process, scientists divide living things into huge groups called **kingdoms**. For example, plants are in one kingdom, while animals are in another. There is some argument among scientists about how many kingdoms there are—at the moment most agree that there are five! Each kingdom is then divided into smaller groups called **phyla** (singular phylum), and the phyla are further divided into **classes**. The next subdivision is into **orders**. Within an order, organisms are grouped into **families** and then into a **genus** (plural genera), which contains a number of closely related **species**. A species is a single kind of organism, such as a mouse or a buttercup. Members of a species can **reproduce** and produce fertile offspring together.

Scientific names

Many living things have a common name, but these can cause confusion when the same organism has different names around the world. To avoid problems, scientists give every species a two-part Latin name, which is the same all over the world. The first part of the scientific name tells you the genus the organism belongs to. The second part tells you the exact species. The coastal redwood tree that grows along the coast of Oregon and California, for example, has the scientific name *Sequoia sempervirens*, while the redwood found in the Sierra Nevada mountains of California is *Sequoia giganteum*.

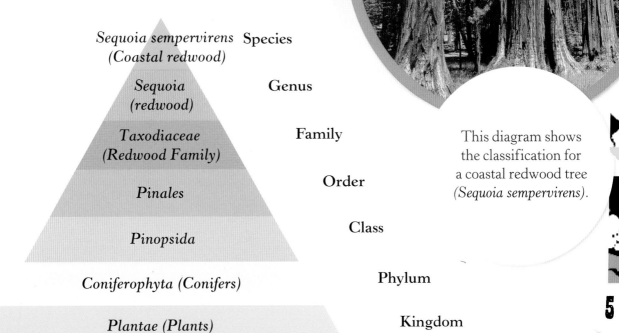

Sequoia sempervirens (Coastal redwood)	Species
Sequoia (redwood)	Genus
Taxodiaceae (Redwood Family)	Family
Pinales	Order
Pinopsida	Class
Coniferophyta (Conifers)	Phylum
Plantae (Plants)	Kingdom

This diagram shows the classification for a coastal redwood tree (*Sequoia sempervirens*).

Nonflowering Plant Divisions

There are more than 30,000 living **species** of nonflowering plants in the plant **kingdom**, grouped into different **divisions**. Scientists have grouped them this way because they think that the species in each division are more closely related to one another than to the species in other divisions. This table shows one **classification** system of nonflowering plants and gives some examples of species in each division.

Division	Examples	Number of species
Seedless plants		
Liverworts	common liverwort, fringed waterwort, braided liverwort	6,500
Hornworts	common hornwort	100
Mosses	burned ground moss, cord moss, silver moss	12,000
Club mosses	shining club moss, running cedar, spike mosses, running pine, Rocky Mountain and quillworts, spike moss, spiny-spored quillwort (lycophytes)	1,000
Horsetails	scouring rush, field horsetail, water horsetail	15
Ferns	adder's tongue, Boston fern, grape fern, tree fern, umbrella fern, maidenhair fern, filmy fern, forking fern	12,000
Whisk ferns	whisk fern, fork fern	5–9
Seed plants		
Conifers	pine, fir, spruce, juniper, cedar, sequoia, redwood	550
Cycads	sago palm, Australian nut palm	100
Gingko	maidenhair tree	1
Gnetophytes	Mormon tea bush, ma huang, tree tumbo, welwitschia	70

Spores

Spores are reproductive **cells**. They are made up of **genetic** material inside a protective covering. Plants that **reproduce** mainly by spores release many spores at one time. New plants can grow from spores under the right conditions—in the presence of water and **nutrients**. Plants that rely mainly on spores to reproduce usually live in moist places, where their spores are likely to grow into new plants.

Seeds

Some plants make **seeds**. A seed contains a tiny plant **embryo**. Food inside a seed helps the embryo grow. The embryo and the food supply are enclosed in a hard outer case that helps keep the embryo from being damaged or drying out. Seed plants can live in drier areas than seedless plants can. They are considered to be better **adapted** to life on land. Long ago, all the plants on Earth lived in water. As plants adapted to life on land, seed-bearing plant species developed.

This photo shows seeds from a Chile pine tree. It can take one to two years for a pine seed to mature and the new tree to begin growing.

This photo shows moss spores magnified 2,000 times. When not magnified, spores look like dust. Plants that rely mainly on spores for reproduction usually make huge numbers of them at a time.

The Plant Kingdom

The plant **kingdom** includes all plants. Most plants make flowers and **fruits**. There are at least 300,000 **species** in the plant kingdom—and around 250,000 of these are flowering plants. The non-flowering plants are the minority.

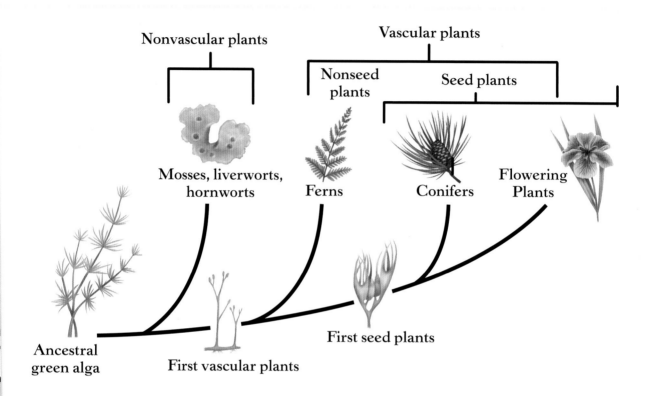

Nonvascular plants

Vascular plants

Nonseed plants

Seed plants

Mosses, liverworts, hornworts

Ferns

Conifers

Flowering Plants

Ancestral green alga

First vascular plants

First seed plants

Plant ancestors

Plants developed from plantlike **organisms** called green **algae**. You may have seen algae growing in a fish aquarium or as seaweed along the shore of a beach. Algae similar to these organisms are thought to be plant **ancestors**.

The first plants probably lived in shallow water or moist regions. Over time, plants **adapted** to life on land and left the water. Most plants live on land today.

This diagram shows one way that scientists think the different **divisions** of plants might be related to one another. Each arm of the diagram shows a group of plants.

Living on land

Living on land posed a number of challenges for plants. To live successfully on land, plants had to be able to get **nutrients**, stay moist, and **reproduce** on land. Plants got nutrients from the soil with the help of **fungi**. Fungi attach to the roots of the plants and bring in nutrients that plants cannot absorb themselves. To conserve water, the plants have an outer waxy coat to help keep water inside them. Plants also **evolved spores** that allowed them to reproduce on land with less water.

Plant life cycles

All plants develop in two main stages. Just as some insects look very different during parts of their life cycle, so do plants. One stage in a plant's life cycle is called the **sporophyte** stage. A sporophyte makes spores. Under the right conditions, each spore can grow into a new plant. In some plants, the sporophytes are tiny. In other plants, the sporophyte is what we think of as the whole plant.

425 million year old plants!

One of the oldest land plants preserved as a **fossil** is *Cooksonia*. Fossils of this small plant—only a couple of centimeters tall—have been dated at about 425 million years old. Using a number of different fossils, scientists have developed models of what this ancient plant looked like. These rare fossils give us an amazing glimpse into the past life of plants.

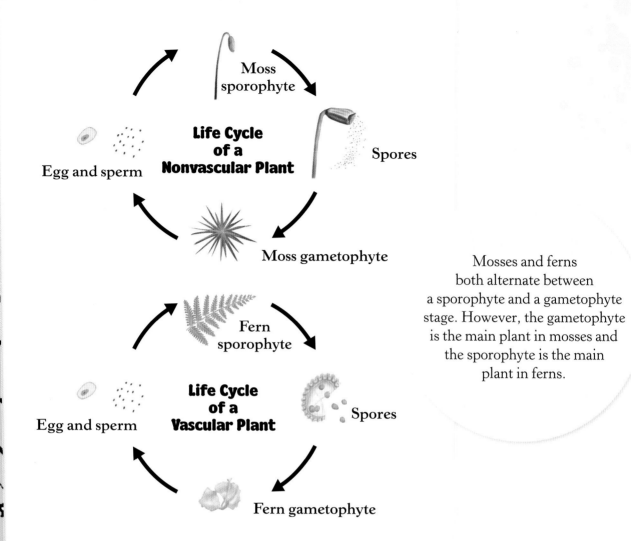

Life Cycle
of a
Nonvascular Plant

Moss sporophyte

Spores

Moss gametophyte

Egg and sperm

Life Cycle
of a
Vascular Plant

Fern sporophyte

Spores

Fern gametophyte

Egg and sperm

Mosses and ferns both alternate between a sporophyte and a gametophyte stage. However, the gametophyte is the main plant in mosses and the sporophyte is the main plant in ferns.

The other stage of a plant's life cycle is called the **gametophyte** stage. Gametophytes **reproduce** by making **eggs** and **sperm**. An egg and a sperm must join together to grow into a new plant. When you look at liverworts, hornworts, and mosses, most of what you see is the gametophyte. The gametophyte stage of ferns is small but **free-living**, while the gametophyte of pine trees and flowering plants is very small and usually grows inside the **sporophyte** part of these plants.

This kind of life cycle is called alternation of generations. The sporophyte produces gametophytes. Gametophytes produce more sporophytes, which, in turn, produce more gametophytes. In this way, plants alternate between sporophyte and gametophyte stages.

It's easy to think of plants having roots, stems, and leaves, but not all of them do. Three **divisions** of plants—the liverworts, the hornworts, and the mosses—do not have stems, leaves, or roots. They don't produce **seeds** for reproduction. And the liverworts and hornworts don't even have **vascular** tissue to carry water and **nutrients** around the plant.

The simplest plants

Liverworts are considered the simplest plants. They are found all over the world, but mostly in tropical areas. Liverworts take in water and nutrients directly through their body. The outside of the green, leaflike part of a liverwort is waxy. The wax keeps water inside the plant and prevents it from drying out.

Rootlike **rhizoids** anchor liverworts to soil, rocks, and trees. Although rhizoids look like roots, they do not take in nutrients or water.

Liverwort—nonvascular plant

- More than 8,000 species
- Found mostly in the Tropics
- Tiny plantlets are held in gemma cups (see photo below)
- In ancient times, people believed the plant could cure liver disease —hence the name!

Like liverworts and hornworts, mosses also lack roots, stems, and leaves. The moss life cycle is similar to that of liverworts and hornworts. For this reason, mosses are often **classified** with liverworts and hornworts.

Soaking up water

Unlike liverworts and hornworts, most mosses have the beginnings of a very simple transport system inside them. Some of their **cells** form tiny tubes, which move water and **nutrients** from one part of the moss plant to another. But it isn't a proper **vascular** system, and they still need to take in most of their water through the surface of their body. This is one of the reasons mosses grow in moist, shady places—these are places where they can easily soak up the water they need to survive. What we think of as a moss plant is actually many small plants growing close together. Living close together allows the plants to hold one another up and to get water.

Earth's carpet

Peat moss, also called *Sphagnum*, covers about three percent of the earth. If you were to make one large rug out of all the peat moss growing on the earth, it would cover almost half of the continental United States. There are probably more peat mosses in the world than any other plant.

The green part of a moss plant is the **gametophyte**. Each thin stalk growing up out of the gametophyte is a **sporophyte**. **Spores** are made in the tiny capsules at the end of each sporophyte.

Living mosses make up the top layer of a bog. Under the living mosses are layers of dead moss plants that grew in the bog in the past. These old layers of dead mosses get pushed down over time, forming dark-colored peat.

When mosses die, their bodies break down and mix with the dirt and dead plants around them. This forms a dry, lightweight, spongy substance called **peat**. In the past, peat was an important fuel for cooking and heating but it is used much less today. The formation of peat from moss is the first step in making **coal**, which is a **fossil fuel**. Today's coal beds were formed by mosses and other non-flowering plants growing in swamps about 300 million years ago. When the plants died, their remains stayed in the swampy water and only partly broke down. Over time, the plant bodies became peat, then coal, as layers of soil and rock lay on top.

Living mosses break down the soil they grow on into nutrients that other plants can use to grow. They also prevent **erosion**, a process in which wind and water wear away soil and its nutrients.

Did you know ... not all mosses are true mosses?

Not all mosses are true mosses. For example, the "moss" that grows on the north side of trees is not even a plant. It's a green **alga** that grows where it is moist. North exposures do not get much sun, so algae usually grow there. But if the west or east side of a tree is blocked by other plants, that side of the tree will not dry out from sun exposure and the algae can grow there, too.

Whisk ferns are the simplest seedless **vascular** plants. They have no roots or leaves. They are made up of stems that split in half like two-pronged forks over and over. This may be one reason whisk ferns are often called fork ferns.

A stem for all jobs

Since whisk ferns do not have leaves and roots, their stems do the jobs that leaves and roots usually do in other plants. The aboveground part of a whisk fern's stem carries out **photosynthesis**. Under the ground, **rhizomes** hold the plant in the soil. Creeping rhizomes sometimes attach whisk ferns to other plants.

Growing in the trees

A number of whisk ferns grow on other plants. Plants that grow on other plants without harming them are called **epiphytes**. In Australia, whisk ferns commonly grow as epiphytes on tree ferns. You can see them hanging from the tree ferns.

The part of the whisk fern that you see here is the sporophyte. The white knobs on the green stems make the spores.

A whisk fern's life

Like other plants, whisk ferns alternate between a **sporophyte** and a **gametophyte** form. In whisk ferns, as in other vascular plants, the gametophyte is about 1 millimeter (0.04 inch) across and only about 3 millimeters (0.1 inch) long—that's a little bit smaller than one grain of rice. Whisk fern gametophytes are also colorless. They usually grow on the trunks of trees or under the ground. Gametophytes **reproduce** by making **eggs** and **sperm**. The eggs and sperm join together to make a new plant. The large green plant body of a whisk fern is the sporophyte. It makes **spores**. Spores can grow into a new plant without joining with any other **cell**.

A system of tubes

If you could see inside most of the plants growing around you, you would see a system of tubes called vascular tissue (as in the buttercup stem below). These tubes are made of chains of hollow cells linked end to end. Like the blood vessels in your body, vascular tissue connects the different parts of a plant's body. It carries water and **nutrients** from one part of the plant to its other parts.

Plants that have a vascular system are able to move water and nutrients quickly. In whisk ferns, the vascular tissue forms a central core in the stem. Nutrients move through linked living plant cells. The tubes that carry water from the roots to the other parts of the plant are made of dead plant cells.

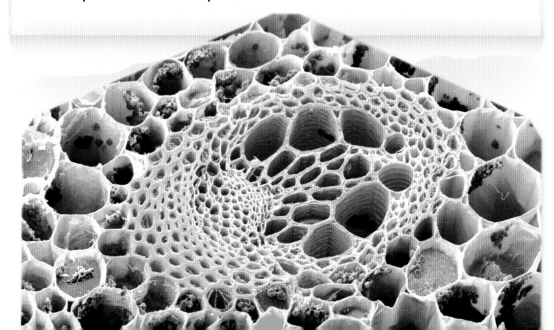

Club mosses, spike mosses, and quillworts are often called **lycophytes**. Many ancient lycophytes were trees as tall as 30 meters (100 feet)—about as tall as a 10-story building. Today's lycophytes tend to be much smaller. They also produce **spores**. Like the whisk ferns, members of this **division** have a **vascular** system. However, unlike whisk ferns, these plants have roots, stems, and leaves.

These plants are vascular, which means they have transport tissues to move water and **nutrients** around the plant body. This is why they were able to grow so large in the past.

Club mosses usually have small leaves that look like needles and cones growing out of stems. The stems form forks at the ends. The roots of club mosses and spike mosses grow under the ground.

Club moss—primitive vascular plants

- About 200 species
- Evergreen plants
- Spores of one type of club moss used in fireworks
- Disagreement among scientists about the classification of lycophytes

Some quillworts are **endangered species**. They live in shallow pools of water that form on top of large granite rocks after it rains. These plants lose their homes when the granite is taken to build things. Cars, vandalism, pollution, fires, littering, and other human activities can also harm quillworts.

Quillworts look like many-legged spiders or spiny sea urchins. They have as many as 30 grassy or spinelike leaves coming from the top of a stem. Their stems are often very short—just a small piece between the leaves and the roots. The stems do not grow tall, although they can grow wider with time.

Extinct lycophytes

Long ago there were two groups of lycophytes: a group of large plants and a group of small ones. Only the group of small lycophytes exists today. The large plants in this division are all **extinct**. The **fossils** of these extinct plants are found in **coal** beds on Earth. These plants grew in warm, humid places. When the plants died, microorganisms broke the plants down into small pieces. Over time, the plant pieces became **fossil fuels**, including coal, just as some mosses did.

Millions of years ago, horsetails were common plants. They grew as tall as trees. Today, horsetails are commonly found along riverbanks and in other moist areas. There are only 15 **species** of horsetails still living today.

Growing tall

Many species of horsetails have become **extinct**. These ancient horsetails were often giant plants. Some were up to 30 meters (100 feet) tall and 1 meter (3 feet) in diameter. That's bigger than many trees growing today.

Not all plants can grow tall. Only plants that have a **vascular** system are able to grow into tall plants. A system of conducting tubes efficiently moves water and **nutrients** to all the parts of the plant. Plants that do not have conducting tubes must be small. They would not be able to move water and food to all their parts if they were large.

Horsetails, like all vascular plants, have rigid stems. Rigid stems also allow plants to grow tall. Plant stems are made rigid by a hard substance, called **cellulose**, in their **cells**. A plant without cellulose would fall over if it grew very tall.

Giant horsetails make up the largest species in the horsetail **genus**. Their stems can be as thick as an adult's wrist, and they can grow as tall as houses. A giant horsetail **sporophyte** is shown here. Like other horsetail plants, the giant horsetail has a stem, leaves, and **cones**. The cones make **spores**.

Gold miners and pot scrubbers

Like other plants, horsetails take in **minerals**, such as gold and silica, from the soil. These minerals form deposits in the plant. The amount of gold found in horsetails is very small. Only 128 grams (4.5 ounces) of gold are found per 907 kilograms (one ton) of plant. However, these minerals have sometimes killed horses that ate a lot of horsetail plants.

Did you know ... horsetails were once used for cleaning?

The smooth scouring rush horsetail shown here is commonly found along riverbanks and roadsides. It also grows in prairies and in many wetlands. Horsetails are very **coarse**. People once used scouring rush horsetails to scrub pots and pans. Horsetails contain large amounts of silica, the main component of sand.

Ferns are probably the most successful and widespread seedless **vascular** plants. The other **divisions** of seedless vascular plants have few living **species** today. Scientists have found **fossils** of some fern species that are now **extinct**.

The parts of a fern

Like other vascular plants, the fern **sporophyte** is the most noticeable part of the plant. It has fanlike leaves called **fronds**. In many ferns, the underside of fronds are lined with clusters of structures that make **spores**. The spores grow into **gametophytes**. Each fern gametophyte has both male and female reproductive structures. This allows **sperm** and **eggs** from the same gametophyte to join and grow into a new fern plant.

If you wanted to find a fern gametophyte growing in a forest, you would have to look carefully. Fern gametophytes are very tiny. They are usually about the size of the nail on your smallest finger—only 0.2–0.8 centimeter (0.08–0.3 inch) long and 0.8 centimeter (0.3 inch) wide.

Most fern stems grow along or just under the ground. These stems are called rhizomes. Fern fronds grow from the stem up from the ground. New fern leaves, called fiddleheads, are curled up. They uncurl as they grow into mature fronds. A few tree ferns have thick stems that look similar to the trunk of a tree.

Hardy spores

Like other plants, ferns have two main stages in their life cycle. Most new ferns come from spores. Many ferns produce spores that have a thick outer wall. This thick wall helps keep the spores from drying out. Some fern spores exist for many years without drying out. When the conditions are favorable, the spore wall cracks. Like a chick hatching from an egg, a fern **rhizome** grows out of the spore and becomes a gametophyte.

Growing on rocks and trees

Ferns are commonly found in moist, shady forests. However, many ferns grow on rocks or trees.

Ferns that grow on rocks are called **epipetric** ferns. Those that grow on trees are called **epiphytic** ferns. Staghorn ferns are epiphytic ferns that are often found in botanical gardens. They grow on the moist bark of other trees and often have antler-shaped fronds. Cliff brakes, maidenhair ferns, and lip ferns grow on rocks and out of rock crevices.

Ferns that grow on rocks and trees have **adapted** in a way that helps them grow successfully in a dry place. For example, the outer layer or skin of the ferns usually has a thick, waxy layer, called a cuticle, which keeps water inside the plant. These ferns sometimes have a lot of hairs or scales on their leaves and stems.

The powdery structures on the underside of this fern frond make spores. Ferns release the spores into the air. When the spores land on moist soil, they are able to grow into new fern plants. This is the main way that ferns **reproduce**.

21

There are two main groups of plants that make **seeds**. Most seed-bearing plants are flowering plants. Flowering plants produce seeds inside **fruits**. **Gymnosperms** are non-flowering seed plants—their seeds are not enclosed in fruits. Gymnosperms make up four of the five **divisions** of seed plants. They were the first plants to have seeds.

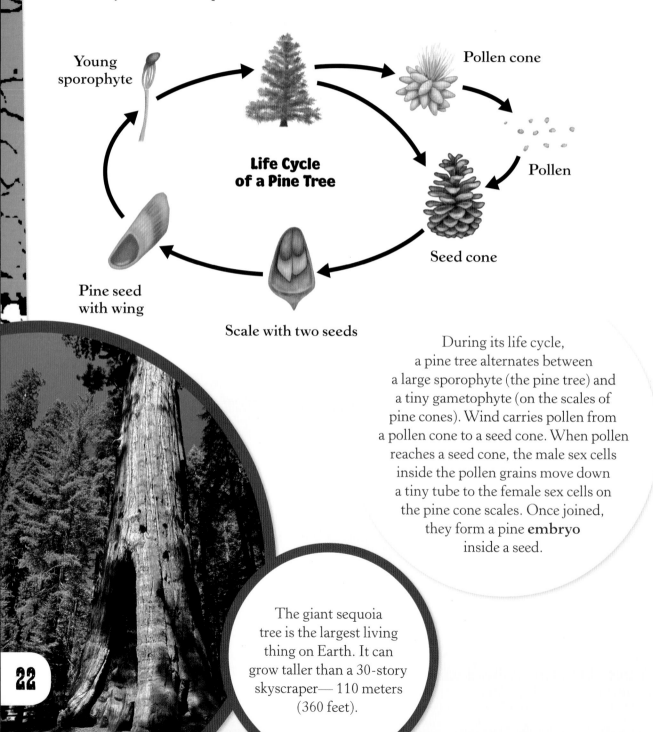

Young sporophyte

Pollen cone

Life Cycle of a Pine Tree

Pollen

Seed cone

Pine seed with wing

Scale with two seeds

During its life cycle, a pine tree alternates between a large sporophyte (the pine tree) and a tiny gametophyte (on the scales of pine cones). Wind carries pollen from a pollen cone to a seed cone. When pollen reaches a seed cone, the male sex cells inside the pollen grains move down a tiny tube to the female sex cells on the pine cone scales. Once joined, they form a pine **embryo** inside a seed.

The giant sequoia tree is the largest living thing on Earth. It can grow taller than a 30-story skyscraper— 110 meters (360 feet).

Naked seeds

The word *gymnosperm* means "naked seed." This means that gymnosperm seeds do not grow in protective structures inside flowers and fruits like those of flowering plants. Many gymnosperms produce seeds inside **cones**. Unlike fruits, cones open up and expose their seeds to the air when they are mature and the environment is favorable.

Pollen

Only seed plants make **pollen**. Pollen is a dustlike substance that contains the male sex cells called **gametes**. In seed plants, these male gametes are carried by wind or animals. Seed plants do not rely on water for the male and female cells to join together.

Gymnosperm life cycle

Like most gymnosperms, pine trees produce cones. The pine tree itself is the **sporophyte** form of the plant. There are separate female and male **gametophyte** forms of the plant. The female gametophyte is found on the scales of a pine cone. Each female gametophyte produces an egg. Pollen cones, which look like smaller, dusty pine cones, make pollen.

Trees can produce large amounts of pollen. You may have even seen yellow pollen dust covering sidewalks or cars. Trees, such as pines, make a large amount of pollen, which ensures that some of it lands on the eggs in pine cones. When wind carries pollen to a pine cone, the male and female gametes can join together and eventually grow into a new sporophyte—a pine tree.

Once the male and female gametes have joined together on the scale of a pine cone, a seed develops. The seed and part of the scale then break away. The part of the scale that stays with the seed looks and works like a wing. It helps a pine seed glide on the wind to a new place so it can grow.

Conifers are the main **gymnosperms**. They include pines, firs, spruces, junipers, cedars, and redwoods. They make up some of the oldest, tallest, and largest plants on Earth. Conifers are trees with needle-shaped leaves. Most stay green all year. Because they stay green all year, these trees are called evergreens.

Cones

Most conifers make two kinds of **cones**. **Seed** cones are female cones. They are usually woody and contain seeds. **Pollen** cones are male and contain clusters of dustlike pollen. The seed cones open when the tree makes pollen. Wind blows the pollen from pollen cones to seed cones. When pollen from a pollen cone lands on a female cone, the male **gametes** in the pollen join with the female gametes inside the cones. This forms a plant **embryo** inside a seed. Seed cones stay on conifers for one or two years. During wet, cold weather, the seed cones close, protecting the seeds within them.

When the weather is favorable for a conifer seed to grow, seed cones open and release seeds with the embryos inside. Often, conifer seeds are attached to paperlike wings that let the wind carry them to new places.

Seed cones usually stay closed until the seeds are ready to grow. In many conifers, such as this lodgepole pine, it takes two years for the seeds to mature.

Growth rings

If you cut down a tree, you are likely to find dark circles inside light circles inside dark circles. These rings correspond to growth cycles. The **cells** of a tree are different in the beginning of a growth cycle than at the end of the growth cycle. The dark rings are formed by dense, small cells that form at the end of the growing season. These dark rings are sometimes called late, or summer, wood. The light rings are made of large cells that form during the start of a growing season. They are sometimes called early, or spring, wood. The place where the spring wood and the summer wood touch makes a ring in the wood. New wood does not usually form during the winter.

Growth rings can be used to determine the age of different kinds of trees. For example, each ring in a conifer tree normally represents one year. These growth rings are called **annual rings**. Annual rings have been used to date ancient Native American structures.

Sometimes, a weather change can affect the way a tree grows. When this happens, the tree might form a **false ring**. Since they are affected by weather patterns, growth rings are also used to study the weather. In tropical areas, conifer trees can have more than one growth ring per year. It might be hard to tell the age of a conifer in a tropical region by its growth rings unless the area has predictable rainy seasons.

Can you guess how old this conifer tree was? Count the annual rings.

Gymnosperms are divided into four **divisions**. The largest and most familiar division of gymnosperms includes 550 **conifers**. Gymnosperms called cycads are often shown in movies set in tropical places. Ginkgo trees, which make up another gymnosperm division, are planted along the streets of cities as decoration and to help reduce air pollution. Cycads, ginkgo, and gnetophytes are each **classified** in their own division.

Cycads

Cycads were probably the earliest gymnosperms. They were common when dinosaurs lived on Earth. Today, there are 100 living cycad **species**. They grow mostly in tropical and subtropical regions. Like conifers, cycads make **cones**. A cycad cone can grow as long as a newborn baby— about 55 centimeters (22 inches) long. Only one species of cycad now grows naturally in the United States—the coontie is still found in Florida.

Ginkgo

The ginkgo division has only one species still living today—the ginkgo, or maidenhair tree. All the other plants in this division are now **extinct**. Some scientists think the ginkgo tree might be the oldest living **seed** plant species alive today.

Cycads have a ring of palmlike leaves that grow like a crown off the top of the stem. Male cycads make pollen cones. Female cycads make seed cones. Wind carries pollen from the pollen cones to the seed cones, just as it does with conifer trees.

Gingko tree—a lonely species

- Deciduous tree
- Often used to line streets as can cope with cold weather, pollution, and little water
- Seed kernel eaten as food in East Asia
- Ginkgo leaf shape used in Asian symbols such as family crests and university seals

The ginkgo tree has fanlike leaves that turn yellow and drop in the fall. For 3,000 years, people have used parts of the ginkgo to treat different medical conditions, including asthma. Today, substances with ginkgo can be found at health food stores.

Gnetophytes

The gnetophyte division of plants has about 70 species. Gnetophytes have flowerlike **reproductive** structures. These plants also have a different type of wood than other gymnosperms have. For these reasons, some scientists think that gnetophytes might be the **ancestors** of flowering plants.

One **genus** of plants in this division, ephedra, also known as ma huang, has been used to treat colds for thousands of years. The active ingredient in the plant, ephedrine, can be found in many cold medications. Another genus of plants in this division is welwitschia. This unusual plant grows only in the Namib Desert in Africa. It has only two long leaves that grow longer over the life of the plant, which is sometimes as long as 100 years.

The number of different types of living **organisms** in the world is often called the **biodiversity**. Sadly, all over the world, **species** of living organisms are becoming **extinct**. This means that these organisms no longer exist on Earth. There are many different reasons for this. Extinction has always happened—some species die out and other species **evolve**. But today people are changing the world in ways that affect all other species.

People are destroying the places where nonflowering plants grow. We are cutting down rain forests and polluting the air and the water. Our use of **fossil fuels**, such as oil and gas, is causing global warming. Global warming is a rise in Earth's average temperature and a change in weather patterns. When the temperature and the weather change, it can have a serious effect on nonflowering plants.

Nonflowering plants have been on Earth a long time. There are clear **fossil** records of them going back hundreds of millions of years.

Nonflowering plants may not be as colorful and pretty as flowering plants, but they are an important part of the rain forest ecosystem.

Plant poachers

People know that animal poachers can hunt an **endangered species** to extinction. But did you realize that plant poachers are doing the same thing? Some of the rarest nonflowering plants are among those threatened. Rare cycads are compact and have interesting shapes, which make them very popular with gardeners. Although they are protected in many places, illegal plant poachers are wiping them out. In South Africa, for example, where many of the world's cycad species can be found, two-thirds of all the species face extinction. Many are sold in South Africa itself, but millions of dollars worth are smuggled into the United States each year. To stop the trade driving these rare plants to extinction, we need to invest more in catching the poachers—and people must stop buying the plants.

But the destruction of habitat by human activities is putting the survival of many species at risk. For example, rain forests are a treasure house of species, with many ferns, mosses, and other species thriving in the warm, wet conditions. Many of these plants have not yet been identified—and some of them may well be very useful to humans. Unfortunately, rain forest is being destroyed at the rate of a small country every day, mainly for new farmland to grow crops such as oil palms or to feed cattle to provide cheap beef for burgers. Many nonflowering plants will become extinct before they have even been identified.

What can be done?

To help prevent nonflowering plants from becoming extinct, people need to look after Earth better. If global warming can be stopped, many species will be saved. It is important to protect the places where nonflowering plants grow—which is almost everywhere. Biodiversity is important—we need as many species of plants as possible for the future.

Glossary

adapted having special features to survive in a habitat

alga (plural is **algae**) plantlike organisms that live in the water

ancestor plant relative that lived millions of years ago

annual ring amount of wood added to a tree during one growing season

bacteria single-celled organism that does not have a nucleus

biodiversity different types of organisms around the world

cell smallest unit of life

cellulose substance produced by plants to strengthen their tissues

class level of classification that contains similar orders

classify group organisms into categories based on their similar characteristics

coal hard, black substance created from the breakdown of plants

coarse harsh or rough

cone scaly fruit of certain trees

conifer cone-bearing tree or shrub

division level of classification that contains similar classes

egg female reproductive structure

embryo structure formed when an egg and a sperm join together

endangered species group of organisms that might die out and be gone forever

epipetric growing on rock

epiphyte plant that grows on another plant or an object above ground, which has no roots in soil

erosion wearing away of earth or rock by high winds or rushing water

evolve change over time

extinct no longer on Earth

false ring tree's additional growth ring produced in a single year due to weather changes

family level of classification that contains similar genera

fossil remains of ancient living organisms, usually formed from bones or shells, found in rocks

fossil fuel substance used for energy that formed from plants living millions of years ago

free-living able to take care of its own needs

frond large leaf or leaflike structure

fruit enlarged female reproductive part of a flowering plant. It contains and protects the seeds of flowering plants.

fungi any of a large group of plantlike organisms that must live on other plants or animals or decaying material

gamete sex cell used for reproduction

gametophyte stage in a plant's life cycle when it makes eggs and sperm

gene substance by which all living things pass on characteristics to the next generation. Species with shared genes are linked by genetics.

genus (plural is **genera**) level of classification grouping between family and species

gymnosperm first seed plants

kingdom level of classification that contains similar phyla or divisions

lycophyte type of club moss

mineral solid substance formed in the earth by nature

nutrient chemical that helps plants grow and carry out life processes

order level of classification that contains similar families

organism living thing

peat dry, lightweight, spongy substance that forms when dead plants break down under certain conditions

photosynthesis process by which plants use carbon dioxide in the air and water and energy from sunlight to make food in the form of sugars

phylum (plural is **phyla**) level of classification that contains similar classes

pollen dustlike particles that contain sperm

reproduce produce another living thing of the same kind

rhizoid rootlike structures that hold liverworts and mosses to soil, rocks, and trees

rhizome underground stem that looks like a root and holds a plant in the soil

seed structure that contains an undeveloped plant and stored food that the plant needs to grow

species level of classification that contains similar organisms

sperm male reproductive structure

spore reproductive structure that contains all the information needed to grow into an adult plant

sporophyte stage in a plant's life cycle when the plant makes spores

vascular having a system of conducting tubes that moves nutrients and water through a plant's body

Find Out More

Burnie, David. *Plant* (e.guides). New York: DK Children, 2006.

Burnie, David. *The Concise Nature Encyclopedia*. Boston, Mass.: Kingfisher, 2006.

Nagle, Jeanne. *Coniferous Forests: An Evergreen World*. New York: Rosen Central, 2009.

Index